Student Edition

FRUIT
GROWS WHERE THE
STREAM
FLOWS

EXPERIENCING THE FRUIT OF
THE SPIRIT IN OUR DAILY LIVES

D1411970

PAUL CHAPPELL

First published in 2007 by Striving Together Publications, a
ministry of Lancaster Baptist Church, Lancaster, CA 93535.
Striving Together Publications is committed to providing tried,
trusted, and proven books that will further equip local churches
to carry out the Great Commission. Your comments and
suggestions are valued.

Striving Together Publications
4020 E. Lancaster Blvd.
Lancaster, CA 93535
800.201.7748

Cover design by Craig Parker and Andrew Jones
Layout by Craig Parker
Edited by Kayla Nelson, Maggie Ruhl, and Sarah Michael
Special thanks to our proofreaders.

ISBN 978-1-59894-027-5

Printed in the United States of America

Table of Contents

Preparing the Soil
PART 1: WHO IS THE HOLY SPIRIT?

Text

Galatians 5:16–23; John 15:1–4; Colossians 2:7

Overview

Many trials and tribulations came during Paul's first missionary journey, yet he faced them with the power of God, continually manifesting love, joy, peace, and faith. Paul's relationship with Christ allowed him to bear these fruits of the Holy Spirit. The Spirit of God who indwelled the Apostle Paul desires to indwell our hearts. We must prepare the soil of our hearts by learning about the Holy Spirit—the source of the fruit of the Spirit.

Lesson Theme

The soil of our hearts must be prepared through the knowledge of the Holy Spirit in order to bear the wonderful fruit of the Spirit.

Introduction

_____

_____

_____

"I am the true vine, and my Father is the husbandman. Every branch in me that beareth not fruit he taketh away: and every branch that beareth fruit, he purgeth it, that it may bring forth more fruit. Now ye are clean through the word which I have spoken unto you. Abide in me, and I in you. As the branch cannot bear fruit of itself, except it abide in the vine; no more can ye, except ye abide in me."—JOHN 15:1–4

I. The ___Gift___ of the Holy Spirit
"Then Peter said unto them, Repent, and be baptized every one of you in the name of Jesus Christ for the remission of sins, and ye shall receive the gift of the Holy Ghost." —ACTS 2:38

"And hope maketh not ashamed; because the love of God is shed abroad in our hearts by the Holy Ghost which is given unto us."—ROMANS 5:5

A. The Holy Spirit Is _____ by Christ
"But the Comforter, which is the Holy Ghost, whom the Father will send in my name, he shall teach you all things, and bring all things to your remembrance, whatsoever I have said unto you."—JOHN 14:26

B. The Holy Spirit Is _____ at Salvation
"Jesus answered, Verily, verily, I say unto thee, Except a man be born of water and of the Spirit, he cannot

enter into the kingdom of God. That which is born of the flesh is flesh; and that which is born of the Spirit is spirit."—JOHN 3:5–6

"What? know ye not that your body is the temple of the Holy Ghost which is in you, which ye have of God, and ye are not your own? For ye are bought with a price: therefore glorify God in your body, and in your spirit, which are God's."—1 CORINTHIANS 6:19–20

C. The Holy Spirit Is the _____ of Our Salvation
"In whom ye also trusted, after that ye heard the word of truth, the gospel of your salvation: in whom also after that ye believed, ye were sealed with that holy Spirit of promise."—EPHESIANS 1:13

"Labour not for the meat which perisheth, but for that meat which endureth unto everlasting life, which the Son of man shall give unto you: for Him hath God the Father sealed."—JOHN 6:27

II. The _Growth_ in the Holy Spirit

A. Growth Is Vital for Avoiding _____

B. Growth Is the _evidence_ of Our Salvation

C. Growth Is Produced as We _walk_ in the _Spirit_
"This I say then, Walk in the Spirit, and ye shall not fulfil the lust of the flesh."—GALATIANS 5:16

III. The _Goodness_ of the Holy Spirit

A. His Character Is _produced_ in You
"By him therefore let us offer the sacrifice of praise to God continually, that is, the fruit of our lips giving thanks to his name."—HEBREWS 13:15

B. His Character Is _witnessed_ by Those around You

Conclusion

_____

_____

_____

"But the fruit of the Spirit is love, joy, peace, longsuffering, gentleness, goodness, faith, Meekness, temperance: against such there is no law."—GALATIANS 5:22–23

Study Questions

1. According to Acts 2:38, when can we receive the Holy Spirit?

2. Why is growing in the Spirit vital for our Christian walk?

3. According to Ephesians 1:13, what does the Holy Spirit do?

4. Is your life bearing spiritual fruit (love, joy, peace, longsuffering, gentleness, goodness, faith, meekness or temperance)? Consider these fruits of the Spirit. Which ones are you consistently bearing in your life right now?

5. How can we have the Holy Spirit's power on a daily basis in order to bear the fruit of the Spirit?

6. When you sin, you are giving in to the flesh (no matter how small the sin is). What precautionary steps can you take to refrain from sin?

7. Think back to the example of the Indian Chief feeding one dog the most. Consider your day-to-day schedule, which do you feed the most—the fruit of the Spirit or the lust of the flesh?

8. Write down what you have done to feed the Spirit today. (Example: Reading God's Word, Attending the Lord's house, etc.)

Memory Verse

"This I say then, Walk in the Spirit, and ye shall not fulfil the lust of the flesh."—Galatians 5:16

Preparing the Soil
PART 2: CHOOSING TO WALK IN THE HOLY SPIRIT

Text
Galatians 5:16; Philippians 1:19–20

Overview
To finish preparing the soil of our hearts, we must choose to walk in the Spirit. The Holy Spirit desires to indwell our hearts and produce fruit in our lives. We are now faced with a choice. We know who the Holy Spirit is, but are we willing to walk in the Spirit?

Lesson Theme
A fruitful Christian life is solely dependent on one choice— will we walk in the Spirit to bear the fruit of the Spirit?

Introduction

_____

_____

_____

I. The _____ of the Believer

A. *Liberty Is Not for* _____

"For, brethren, ye have been called unto liberty; only use not liberty for an occasion to the flesh, but by love serve one another."—GALATIANS 5:13

"For the grace of God that bringeth salvation hath appeared to all men, Teaching us that, denying ungodliness and worldly lusts, we should live soberly, righteously, and godly, in this present world; Looking for that blessed hope, and the glorious appearing of the great God and our Saviour Jesus Christ."—TITUS 2:11–13

B. *Liberty Is for* _____ *Others*

"For, brethren, ye have been called unto liberty; only use not liberty for an occasion to the flesh, but by love serve one another. For all the law is fulfilled in one word, even in this; Thou shalt love thy neighbour as thyself."—GALATIANS 5:13–14

"And he said unto me, My grace is sufficient for thee: for my strength is made perfect in weakness. Most gladly therefore will I rather glory in my infirmities,

that the power of Christ may rest upon me."
—2 CORINTHIANS 12:9

"*Let your speech be alway with grace, seasoned with salt, that ye may know how ye ought to answer every man.*"—COLOSSIANS 4:6

II. The Walk of the _____

A. *It Is a Walk in the* _____

B. *It Is a* _____ *Walk*
"*But if ye be led of the Spirit, ye are not under the law.*"—GALATIANS 5:18

"*Likewise reckon ye also yourselves to be dead indeed unto sin, but alive unto God through Jesus Christ our Lord. Let not sin therefore reign in your mortal body, that ye should obey it in the lusts thereof.*"
—ROMANS 6:11–12

III. The _____ within Each Christian

A. *The* _____ *of the Flesh*
"*Jesus answered them, Verily, verily, I say unto you, Whosoever committeth sin is the servant of sin.*"
—JOHN 8:34

"Knowing this, that our old man is crucified with him, that the body of sin might be destroyed, that henceforth we should not serve sin."—ROMANS 6:6

B. The _____ of the Spirit
"But the natural man receiveth not the things of the Spirit of God: for they are foolishness unto him: neither can he know them, because they are spiritually discerned."—1 CORINTHIANS 2:14

"But we all, with open face beholding as in a glass the glory of the Lord, are changed into the same image from glory to glory, even as by the Spirit of the Lord."
—2 CORINTHIANS 3:18

Conclusion

_____

_____

_____

"Likewise, ye younger, submit yourselves unto the elder. Yea, all of you be subject one to another, and be clothed with humility: for God resisteth the proud, and giveth grace to the humble."
— 1 PETER 5:5

Study Questions

1. What choice are we given in Galatians 5:16?

2. What is liberty intended to be used for? How could we use liberty in a wrong way?

3. Describe the meaning of the word walk in Galatians 5:16.

4. Do you easily make decisions, or would you rather others make them? Explain what it would take to make the crucial decision of walking in the Spirit.

5. Right now, are you walking in the Spirit? Consider your lifestyle. Is there anything hindering you from walking more in the Spirit? (Example: not enough time spent with God, easily succumbing to the flesh, etc.)

6. When do you become the servant of sin? (John 8:34)

7. Picture yourself completely yielded to God, walking in His Spirit. As you picture this, describe what your life would look like.

8. Compare this picture to your life now. Is it right to choose to walk in the Spirit now that you have envisioned what God can do through you?

Memory Verse

"For, brethren, ye have been called unto liberty; only use not liberty for an occasion to the flesh, but by love serve one another."—GALATIANS 5:13

The Fruit of Love

Text

Galatians 5:22–23; John 15:5; 1 John 4:16;
1 Corinthians 13:1–8

Overview

The Bible says that love is the first fruit of the Spirit—the first characteristic that flows from God into the life of a believer. The fruit of the Spirit illustrates the Christian's connection to the vine—Jesus Christ. When you are connected to Christ, Who is Love, the power to demonstrate this attribute in your daily life becomes possible.

Lesson Theme

A Christian walking in the Spirit will experience the fruit of love—described and displayed in the Scriptures as being above all things.

Introduction

_____

_____

_____

"Hereby perceive we the love of God, because he laid down his life for us: and we ought to lay down our lives for the brethren."
—1 JOHN 3:16

I. The _____ of Love

A. *Defined in _____*

B. *Defined in _____*
"He that loveth not knoweth not God; for God is love."
—1 JOHN 4:8

"The LORD hath appeared of old unto me, saying, Yea, I have loved thee with an everlasting love: therefore with lovingkindness have I drawn thee."—JEREMIAH 31:3

"...when Jesus knew that his hour was come that he should depart out of this world unto the Father, having loved his own (the disciples) which were in the world, he loved them unto the end."—JOHN 13:1

II. The _____ of Love

A. *The _____ of Biblical Love*

    1.   LOVE IS _____

    2.   LOVE IS _____
        "Finally, be ye all of one mind, having compassion one of another, love as brethren, be pitiful, be courteous."—1 PETER 3:8

B. **The _____ of Biblical Love**

    1.   LOVE IS NOT _____

    2.   LOVE DOES NOT _____

    3.   LOVE IS NOT _____

C. **The _____ of Biblical Love**

    1.   LOVE DOES NOT _____
        UNBECOMINGLY

    2.   LOVE DOES NOT _____ ITS OWN
        "Look not every man on his own things, but every man also on the things of others."
        —PHILIPPIANS 2:4

    3.   LOVE IS NOT EASILY _____
        "Who, when he was reviled, reviled not again; when he suffered, he threatened not; but committed himself to him that judgeth righteously."
        —1 PETER 2:23

        "...Father, forgive them; for they know not what they do...." —LUKE 23:34

4. **LOVE DOES NOT** _____

   "To wit, that God was in Christ, reconciling the world unto himself, not imputing their trespasses unto them; and hath committed unto us the word of reconciliation."—2 CORINTHIANS 5:19

III. The _____ of Love

A. _____ *Love Is Displayed through Giving*

"Finally, be ye all of one mind, having compassion one of another, love as brethren, be pitiful, be courteous:"
—1 PETER 3:8

"If a man say, I love God, and hateth his brother, he is a liar: for he that loveth not his brother whom he hath seen, how can he love God whom he hath not seen? And this commandment have we from him, That he who loveth God love his brother also."—1 JOHN 4:20–21

B. _____ *Love Was Displayed through Giving*

Conclusion

_____

_____

_____

"But God commendeth his love toward us, in that, while we were yet sinners, Christ died for us."—ROMANS 5:8

Study Questions

1. Define the word *Eros* and tell how it is evident in our culture today.

2. Define the word *Philos* and explain the concerns of this type of love.

3. Define the word *Agape* and give a detailed account of the person who demonstrated this love and how He did it.

4. Define the word *love* according to 1 John 4:8.

5. According to 1 Corinthians 13, love is patient. When you tell your friends you love them, yet you get very impatient with them, what message are you sending them?

6. What should your first reaction be if a friend or family member, whom you love, just received a brand new car from his boss?

7. Explain why a child of God should be in constant display of biblical love.

8. We can display our love through giving in what three areas? Which of these areas is your weakest? What steps can you take to strengthen that area?

Memory Verse

"But God commendeth his love toward us, in that, while we were yet sinners, Christ died for us."—ROMANS 5:8

The Fruit of Joy

Text

Galatians 5:22–23; Philippians 4:4; Romans 14:17;
1 Thessalonians 1:6

Overview

People of every kind are searching for joy in all the wrong places—riches, materialism, and selfish gain. The happiness this world offers is only temporal, but the joy of the Holy Spirit lasts for eternity. The Scripture in this lesson guides its readers to a healthy examination of what joy is and how to obtain it.

Lesson Theme

A Christian walking in the Spirit will experience the fruit of joy through sufferings, trials, and persecutions, as well as through the blessings of life.

Introduction

_____

_____

_____

I. The _____ for Our Joy

A. *Joy Begins at _____*

"*Now the God of hope fill you with all joy and peace in believing, that ye may abound in hope, through the power of the Holy Ghost.*"—ROMANS 15:13

"*Notwithstanding in this rejoice not, that the spirits are subject unto you; but rather rejoice, because your names are written in heaven.*"—LUKE 10:20

B. *Joy Is the _____ of the _____*

"*For the kingdom of God is not meat and drink; but righteousness, and peace, and joy in the Holy Ghost.*"—ROMANS 14:17

"*Delight thyself also in the LORD; and he shall give thee the desires of thine heart.*"—PSALM 37:4

II. The _____ of Our Joy

A. *There Is Joy in _____*

"*Wherein ye greatly rejoice, though now for a season, if need be, ye are in heaviness through manifold temptations:*"—1 PETER 1:6–8

"Therefore being justified by faith, we have peace with God through our Lord Jesus Christ: By whom also we have access by faith into this grace wherein we stand, and rejoice in hope of the glory of God. And not only so, but we glory in tribulations also: knowing that tribulation worketh patience; And patience, experience; and experience, hope:" —Romans 5:1–4

B. There Is Joy in _____

"My brethren, count it all joy when ye fall into divers temptations; Knowing this, that the trying of your faith worketh patience. But let patience have her perfect work, that ye may be perfect and entire, wanting nothing."—James 1:2–4

C. There Is Joy in _____

"Blessed are they which are persecuted for righteousness' sake: for theirs is the kingdom of heaven. Blessed are ye, when men shall revile you, and persecute you, and shall say all manner of evil against you falsely, for my sake. Rejoice, and be exceeding glad: for great is your reward in heaven: for so persecuted they the prophets which were before you."—Matthew 5:10–12

III. The _____ of Our Joy

A. Joy Is Revealed in Our _____

"Make a joyful noise unto the Lord...."—Psalm 100:1

"Is any among you afflicted? let him pray. Is any merry? let him sing psalms."—James 5:13

B. Joy Is Revealed in Our _____

"But none of these things move me, neither count I my life dear unto myself, so that I might finish my course with joy, and the ministry, which I have received of the Lord Jesus, to testify the gospel of the grace of God."—ACTS 20:24

C. Joy Is Revealed in Our _____

"They that sow in tears shall reap in joy. He that goeth forth and weepeth, bearing precious seed, shall doubtless come again with rejoicing, bringing his sheaves with him."—PSALM 126:5–6

D. Joy Is Revealed in Our _____

"How that in a great trial of affliction the abundance of their joy and their deep poverty abounded unto the riches of their liberality. For to their power, I bear record, yea, and beyond their power they were willing of themselves;"—2 CORINTHIANS 8:2–3

Conclusion

_____

_____

_____

"Looking unto Jesus the author and finisher of our faith; who for the joy that was set before him endured the cross, despising the shame, and is set down at the right hand of the throne of God."—HEBREWS 12:2

Study Questions

1. According to Philippians 4:4, how often are we supposed to have joy?

2. Where does joy begin?

3. According to Nehemiah 8:10, the joy of the Lord is our what?

4. In what four areas is joy revealed in our lives?

5. How can you experience joy through suffering?

6. God says if you suffer in His name it is a privilege. When was the last time you suffered for Christ? How did this situation grow you closer to Him?

7. When the offering plate is passed down your row, do you have sincere gladness in your heart that you are able to give to the work of the Lord? If your answer is no, consider your source of joy. In what areas do you need to yield to the source of this fruit—the Holy Spirit?

8. Describe the moment you received the joy of salvation.

Memory Verse

"Looking unto Jesus the author and finisher of our faith; who for the joy that was set before him endured the cross, despising the shame, and is set down at the right hand of the throne of God."—HEBREWS 12:2

The Fruit of Peace

Text
Galatians 5:22–23; Romans 5:1

Overview
We live in a very stressful world. Through the hustle and bustle of life, people are longing for a peaceful moment because a life of peace seems too far out of reach. God's Word shows us how we can experience more than just a moment of peace. God offers a life of peace to every person. No more wishing for that getaway to enjoy "peace"—we can enjoy true peace right now and throughout eternity.

Lesson Theme
God wants us to experience the fruit of peace in relation with Him, with ourselves, and with others.

Introduction

_____

_____

_____

I. Be at Peace with _____

"Peace I leave with you, my peace I give unto you: not as the world giveth, give I unto you. Let not your heart be troubled, neither let it be afraid."—JOHN 14:27

A. Peace with _____ Is _____

"These things I have spoken unto you, that in me ye might have peace. In the world ye shall have tribulation: but be of good cheer; I have overcome the world."—JOHN 16:33

"Those things, which ye have both learned, and received, and heard, and seen in me, do: and the God of peace shall be with you."—PHILIPPIANS 4:9

B. Peace Is Available through _____

"Wherefore, as by one man sin entered into the world, and death by sin; and so death passed upon all men, for that all have sinned:"—ROMANS 5:12

"And, having made peace through the blood of his cross, by him to reconcile all things unto himself; by him, I say, whether they be things in earth, or things in heaven."—COLOSSIANS 1:20

II. Be at Peace _____

A. *Peace Is a* _____ *of the* _____

"Be careful for nothing; but in every thing by prayer and supplication with thanksgiving let your requests be made known unto God. And the peace of God, which passeth all understanding, shall keep your hearts and minds through Christ Jesus."—PHILIPPIANS 4:6–7

B. *God's Peace Is* _____ *by the Word of God*

"Great peace have they which love thy law: and nothing shall offend them."—PSALM 119:165

III. Be at Peace in _____

"Follow peace with all men, and holiness, without which no man shall see the Lord:"—HEBREWS 12:14

A. *In Our* _____

"And let the peace of God rule in your hearts, to the which also ye are called in one body; and be ye thankful."—COLOSSIANS 3:15

B. *In Our* _____

"For God is not the author of confusion, but of peace, as in all churches of the saints."—1 CORINTHIANS 14:33

C. *In Our* _____

"And the way of peace have they not known: There is no fear of God before their eyes."—ROMANS 3:17–18

"I exhort therefore, that, first of all, supplications, prayers, intercessions, and giving of thanks, be made for all men; For kings, and for all that are in authority; that we may lead a quiet and peaceable life in all godliness and honesty. For this is good and acceptable in the sight of God our Saviour; Who will have all men to be saved, and to come unto the knowledge of the truth."—1 TIMOTHY 2:1–4

Conclusion

_____

_____

_____

Study Questions

1. How is the peace of God available to all men?

2. What does the Old Testament word for peace, shalom, mean?

3. Who does the peace of God come from?

4. What three areas in your life need the presence of peace?

5. In your own words, describe what peace means to you.

6. What areas in your life lack peace? (Job, family, specific relationships…)

7. What does Romans 3:17–18 say about the lack of peace in our world? How can we as individuals bring peace to our nation?

8. The areas in your life that lack peace are most likely your areas of worry. How can you change the act of worrying about something into the act of trusting in Someone? (Example: Instead of worrying about a bill being paid, how can you trust God to provide? Answer: Begin praying fervently, etc.)

Memory Verse

"Peace I leave with you, my peace I give unto you: not as the world giveth, give I unto you. Let not your heart be troubled, neither let it be afraid."—JOHN 14:27

The Fruit of Longsuffering

Text
Galatians 5:22–23; Exodus 34:6; Numbers 14:18; Ephesians 4:26

Overview
Longsuffering played an important role in the life of Christ, and if we are to be conformed to His image, it must play a big role in our lives as well. The following study of longsuffering shows how we can implement this fruit of the Spirit into our lives.

Lesson Theme
The importance of longsuffering in the life of a believer is revealed during times of trial, testing, and success.

Introduction

_____

_____

_____

I. The _____ of Longsuffering

"But in all things approving ourselves as the ministers of God, in much patience, in afflictions, in necessities, in distresses." —2 Corinthians 6:4

"Take, my brethren, the prophets, who have spoken in the name of the Lord, for an example of suffering affliction, and of patience."—James 5:10

A. We Persevere Because of God's _____

"For whom the Lord loveth he chasteneth, and scourgeth every son whom he receiveth. If ye endure chastening, God dealeth with you as with sons; for what son is he whom the father chaseneth not?"—Hebrews 12:6–7

"It is good for me that I have been afflicted; that I might learn thy statutes."—Psalm 119:71

B. We Persevere Because of God's _____

"And we know that all things work together for good to them that love God, to them who are the called according to his purpose. For whom he did foreknow, he also did predestinate to be conformed to the image of his Son, that he might be the firstborn among many brethren."—Romans 8:28–29

II. The _____ of Longsuffering

A. With Our _____

"*Let no corrupt communication proceed out of your mouth, but that which is good to the use of edifying, that it may minister grace unto the hearers.*"
—EPHESIANS 4:29

B. With _____ around _____

"*Charity suffereth long, and is kind; charity envieth not; charity vaunteth not itself, is not puffed up.*"
—1 CORINTHIANS 13:4

"*I therefore, the prisoner of the Lord, beseech you that ye walk worthy of the vocation wherewith ye are called, With all lowliness and meekness, with longsuffering, forbearing one another in love; Endeavouring to keep the unity of the Spirit in the bond of peace.*"
—EPHESIANS 4:1–3

"*Who, when he was reviled, reviled not again; when he suffered, he threatened not; but committed himself to him that judgeth righteously:*"—1 PETER 2:23

III. The _____ of Longsuffering

A. The Deliverance of _____

"*The Lord is not slack concerning his promise, as some men count slackness; but is longsuffering to us-ward, not willing that any should perish, but that all should come to repentance.*"—2 PETER 3:9

"Howbeit for this cause I obtained mercy, that in me first Jesus Christ might shew forth all longsuffering, for a pattern to them which should hereafter believe on him to life everlasting."—1 Timothy 1:16

B. The Deliverance of the _____

"Nevertheless we, according to his promise, look for new heavens and a new earth, wherein dwelleth righteousness. Wherefore, beloved, seeing that ye look for such things, be diligent that ye may be found of him in peace, without spot, and blameless. And account that the longsuffering of our Lord is salvation; even as our beloved brother Paul also according to the wisdom given unto him hath written unto you:"
—2 Peter 3:13–15

Conclusion

_____

_____

_____

"Be ye also patient; stablish your hearts: for the coming of the Lord draweth nigh."—James 5:8

Study Questions

1. What is the definition of longsuffering?

2. What are two reasons to persevere?

3. Longsuffering delivers us in what two ways?

4. Can we use self-determination to gain longsuffering? Why or why not?

5. For what three reasons does God bring trials into our lives? Looking back on your most recent trial, can you see why God allowed it into your life? Explain why?

6. Why does God want you to influence your family during difficult times? What is the right way to influence them and what is the wrong way to influence them when a trial comes?

7. What is your primary vocation or calling in this life? What does Ephesians 4:1–3 say about this calling?

8. What are some areas in your life in which you could immediately implement longsuffering? List them. How might your influence change in each area if you choose to exhibit longsuffering? Comment next to each item on your previous list.

Memory Verse

"*The Lord is not slack concerning his promise, as some men count slackness; but is longsuffering to us-ward, not willing that any should perish, but that all should come to repentance.*"—2 PETER 3:9

The Fruit of Gentleness

Text
Galatians 5:22–23; 1 Thessalonians 2:7; Romans 3:10–12

Overview
Gentleness does not come naturally; it must be learned and practiced through the power of the Holy Spirit. This lesson will teach you three truths about gentleness that you must know in order to apply it to every situation that comes into your life.

Lesson Theme
The perfect example of gentleness is Jesus Christ. Christians can follow His example and express gentleness in scriptural ways through the empowerment of the Holy Spirit.

Introduction

_____

_____

_____

I. The _____ of Gentleness

"O praise the Lord, all ye nations: praise him, all ye people. For his merciful kindness is great toward us: and the truth of the Lord endureth for ever. Praise ye the Lord."—PSALM 117:1–2

A. The _____ of Jesus

"For even hereunto were ye called: because Christ also suffered for us, leaving us an example, that ye should follow his steps: Who did no sin, neither was guile found in his mouth: Who, when he was reviled, reviled not again; when he suffered, he threatened not; but committed himself to him that judgeth righteously: Who his own self bare our sins in his own body on the tree, that we, being dead to sins, should live unto righteousness: by whose stripes ye were healed." —1 PETER 2:21–24

B. The _____ of Jesus

"But after that the kindness and love of God our Saviour toward man appeared, Not by works of righteousness which we have done, but according to his mercy he saved us, by the washing of regeneration, and renewing of the Holy Ghost; Which he shed on us abundantly through Jesus Christ our Saviour; That

being justified by his grace, we should be made heirs according to the hope of eternal life."—TITUS 3:4–7

"That in the ages to come he might shew the exceeding riches of his grace in his kindness toward us through Christ Jesus. For by grace are ye saved through faith; and that not of yourselves: it is the gift of God: Not of works, lest any man should boast."—EPHESIANS 2:7–9

"Or despisest thou the riches of his goodness and forbearance and longsuffering; not knowing that the goodness of God leadeth thee to repentance?"—ROMANS 2:4

II. The _____ of Gentleness

A. *Through* _____
"Look not every man on his own things, but every man also on the things of others. Let this mind be in you, which was also in Christ Jesus:"—PHILIPPIANS 2:4–5

B. *Through* _____
"Rejoice with them that do rejoice, and weep with them that weep."—ROMANS 12:15

C. *Through* _____
"Faithful are the wounds of a friend; but the kisses of an enemy are deceitful."—PROVERBS 27:6

D. *Through* _____
"As we have therefore opportunity, let us do good unto all men, especially unto them who are of the household of faith."—GALATIANS 6:10

III. The _____ of Gentleness

A. We Are _____ by the Spirit

"And be not drunk with wine, wherein is excess; but be filled with the Spirit;"—EPHESIANS 5:18

"Put on therefore, as the elect of God, holy and beloved, bowels of mercies, kindness, humbleness of mind, meekness, longsuffering; Forbearing one another, and forgiving one another, if any man have a quarrel against any: even as Christ forgave you, so also do ye."—COLOSSIANS 3:12–13

B. We Are _____ by the Testimony of Jesus

"And grieve not the holy Spirit of God, whereby ye are sealed unto the day of redemption. Let all bitterness, and wrath, and anger, and clamour, and evil speaking, be put away from you, with all malice: And be ye kind one to another, tenderhearted, forgiving one another, even as God for Christ's sake hath forgiven you."
—EPHESIANS 4:30–32

Conclusion

_____

_____

_____

Study Questions

1. What is the definition of gentleness?

2. According to 1 Peter 2:21–24, what was Christ's reaction to His inflicted suffering?

3. What four ways can we channel gentleness into our daily life routine?

4. Where is the first place the power of the Holy Spirit's gentleness should be exhibited?

5. Just as Jesus showed compassion by offering salvation to sinners, how can we show compassion to others?

6. Who in your church needs sympathy? How can you exemplify gentleness by showing sympathy to them?

7. This week, be spontaneous with your family. Write down one idea you can surprise them with.

8. What are three ways you can display the fruit of gentleness this week—in your home, community, and church? List them and how you will follow through in applying gentleness to each one.

Memory Verse

"And be not drunk with wine, wherein is excess; but be filled with the Spirit;"—EPHESIANS 5:18

The Fruit of Goodness

Text

Galatians 5:22–23; Ephesians 5:8–10; Galatians 6:10; Psalm 100:5

Overview

The Holy Spirit's fruit of goodness is a much needed characteristic. Jesus Christ displayed goodness. We can learn from His example and reveal His goodness to a lost and dying world.

Lesson Theme

The Holy Spirit's fruit of goodness will reign in the life of the believer who genuinely accepts God's good gift of salvation and shares it with the lost world.

Introduction

_____

_____

_____

"Every good gift and every perfect gift is from above, and cometh down from the Father of lights, with whom is no variableness, neither shadow of turning."—JAMES 1:17

I. _____ Your Need for God's Goodness

A. *Our Original _____ Is Not _____*

"Wherefore, as by one man sin entered into the world, and death by sin; and so death passed upon all men, for that all have sinned."—ROMANS 5:12

"They are all gone out of the way, they are together become unprofitable; there is none that doeth good, no, not one."—ROMANS 3:12

B. *We Cannot Produce True _____*

"For I know that in me (that is, in my flesh,) dwelleth no good thing: for to will is present with me; but how to perform that which is good I find not."—ROMANS 7:18

"But we are all as an unclean thing, and all our righteousnesses are as filthy rags; and we all do fade as a leaf; and our iniquities, like the wind, have taken us away."—ISAIAH 64:6

II. _____ Christ as Your Saviour

A. You Will Be _____ of His Spirit

"Jesus answered, Verily, verily, I say unto thee, Except a man be born of water and of the Spirit, he cannot enter into the kingdom of God. That which is born of the flesh is flesh; and that which is born of the Spirit is spirit. Marvel not that I said unto thee, Ye must be born again."—JOHN 3:5–7

"That ye put off concerning the former conversation the old man, which is corrupt according to the deceitful lusts; And be renewed in the spirit of your mind; And that ye put on the new man, which after God is created in righteousness and true holiness."
—EPHESIANS 4:22–24

B. You Will _____ of His Divine _____

"According as his divine power hath given unto us all things that pertain unto life and godliness, through the knowledge of him that hath called us to glory and virtue: Whereby are given unto us exceeding great and precious promises: that by these ye might be partakers of the divine nature, having escaped the corruption that is in the world through lust."—2 PETER 1:3–4

III. _____ the Goodness of God to a Lost World

"For ye were sometimes darkness, but now are ye light in the Lord: walk as children of light: (For the fruit of the Spirit is in all goodness and righteousness and

49

truth;) Proving what is acceptable unto the Lord."
—EPHESIANS 5:8–10

A. Goodness Is Found in the _____
"*Wherewithal shall a young man cleanse his way? by taking heed thereto according to thy word.*"
—PSALM 119:9

"*This is my comfort in my affliction: for thy word hath quickened me.*"—PSALM 119:50

"*Order my steps in thy word: and let not any iniquity have dominion over me.*"—PSALM 119:133

"*My tongue shall speak of thy word: for all thy commandments are righteousness.*"—PSALM 119:172

B. Goodness Is _____ **through a** _____ **with Christ**
"*Let your light so shine before men, that they may see your good works, and glorify your Father which is in heaven.*"—MATTHEW 5:16

Conclusion

_____

_____

_____

"*Having your conversation honest among the Gentiles: that, whereas they speak against you as evildoers, they may by your good works, which they shall behold, glorify God in the day of visitation.*"—1 PETER 2:12

Study Questions

1. What cleansing agent has God provided to restore vitality in our relationships?

2. Write down a couple of ways the world interprets the meaning of good.

3. How does our sin nature relate to a worm and an apple?

4. What does Romans 7:18 say about our capability of producing goodness?

5. Goodness is found in the Word of God. How much time have you spent reading the Bible in the past seven days? Write down one truth you remember from your Bible reading that helps you have the spirit of goodness in your everyday life.

6. When you say, "I didn't have dessert—I was good," how does this differ from your saying, "God is so good"? Is there a difference between the two ways the word good is used, if so what is it?

7. To obtain the fruit of goodness, we must have the Holy Spirit indwelling in us. According to the Bible, how do we get the Holy Spirit to live inside of us? If you have the Holy Spirit living inside of you, describe how it took place.

8. Good works do not save us, but they are a manifestation of God's goodness in our lives. What good works have you been involved in recently?

Memory Verse

"Let your light so shine before men, that they may see your good works, and glorify your Father which is in heaven."
—MATTHEW 5:16

The Fruit of Faithfulness

Text
Galatians 5:22–23; Hebrews 10:23–25; Matthew 25:14–21

Overview
The Holy Spirit's fruit of faith naturally produces faithfulness—God's one universal requirement for Christians. Being rooted in Christ enables us to bring forth this fruit, and through biblical principles and examples, we will see how to grow the fruit of faithfulness more abundantly in our lives through the power of the Spirit.

Lesson Theme
We are commanded through the Scriptures to exemplify this fruit of the Spirit in specific areas. These areas of faithfulness are important to understand to remain loyal and true to God on this journey of life.

Introduction

_____

_____

_____

I. _____ in Faithfulness

A. _____ Is Faithful

"Know therefore that the LORD thy God, he is God, the faithful God, which keepeth covenant and mercy with them that love him and keep his commandments to a thousand generations:"—DEUTERONOMY 7:9

"There hath no temptation taken you but such as is common to man: but God is faithful, who will not suffer you to be tempted above that ye are able; but will with the temptation also make a way to escape, that ye may be able to bear it."—1 CORINTHIANS 10:13

"If we confess our sins, he is faithful and just to forgive us our sins, and to cleanse us from all unrighteousness."—1 JOHN 1:9

B. _____ Is Faithful

"For ever, O LORD, thy word is settled in heaven."—PSALM 119:89

"If we believe not, yet he abideth faithful: he cannot deny himself."—2 TIMOTHY 2:13

II. _____ to Be Faithful

A. Faithful to Your _____

"And whatsoever ye do, do it heartily, as to the Lord, and not unto men:"—COLOSSIANS 3:23

B. Faithful to Your _____

"Husbands, love your wives, even as Christ also loved the church, and gave himself for it; That he might sanctify and cleanse it with the washing of water by the word."—EPHESIANS 5:25–26

C. Faithful in Your _____

"He that is faithful in that which is least is faithful also in much: and he that is unjust in the least is unjust also in much. If therefore ye have not been faithful in the unrighteous mammon, who will commit to your trust the true riches? And if ye have not been faithful in that which is another man's, who shall give you that which is your own?"—LUKE 16:10–12

D. Faithful in Your _____

"Not forsaking the assembling of ourselves together, as the manner of some is; but exhorting one another: and so much the more, as ye see the day approaching."
—HEBREWS 10:25

III. _____ of Faithfulness

"Moreover it is required in stewards, that a man be found faithful. But with me it is a very small thing that I should be judged of you, or of man's judgment: yea, I judge not mine own self. For I know nothing by myself; yet am I

not hereby justified: but he that judgeth me is the Lord. Therefore judge nothing before the time, until the Lord come, who both will bring to light the hidden things of darkness, and will make manifest the counsels of the hearts: and then shall every man have praise of God."
—1 CORINTHIANS 4:2–5

A. We All Have Different _____

B. We Will Be _____ **According to Our Faithfulness**
"Fear none of those things which thou shalt suffer: behold, the devil shall cast some of you into prison, that ye may be tried; and ye shall have tribulation ten days: be thou faithful unto death, and I will give thee a crown of life."—REVELATION 2:10

Conclusion

_____

_____

_____

Study Questions

1. What does faith produce?

2. What does 1 John 1:9 say God is faithful in?

3. Why are people attracted to Old Faithful in Yellowstone National Park? Would people be drawn to you because of your faithfulness? Why or why not?

4. We are exhorted to be faithful in what four areas?

5. Describe the short supply of faithfulness we have in our world today. Give examples.

6. In what three different contexts in the book of Galatians is the word faith used? Write out each meaning and ask yourself if you have the three types of faith the Bible speaks of in Galatians.

7. Why is it important to be faithful to your workplace? What does having an unfaithful testimony say to those around you?

8. According to the parable of the talents, God gave each man an opportunity to be faithful. What areas has God given you in which to practice faithfulness? List them and consider how you can be more faithful in each opportunity.

Memory Verse

"Moreover it is required in stewards, that a man be found faithful."—1 CORINTHIANS 4:2

The Fruit of Meekness

Text

Galatians 5:22–23; Ephesians 4:2; Psalm 147:6;
Colossians 3:12–13

Overview

Many people believe that meekness is defined by a woman who speaks in a quiet voice or a person who is "weak." But that is not the true definition of meekness. Through God's Word, true meekness reveals itself, its service, and its significance in the life of a believer.

Lesson Theme

The fruit of meekness played an important role in the life of Christ as it should also in the life of Christians. The fruit of meekness comes from a specific source, has a purposed service, and results in true significance.

Introduction

_____

_____

_____

I. The _____ of Meekness

A. Meekness Is _____ by the Holy Spirit
"The meek will he guide in judgment: and the meek will he teach his way."—Psalm 25:9

"The meek shall eat and be satisfied: they shall praise the Lord that seek him: your heart shall live for ever."—Psalm 22:26

B. Meekness Is _____ by Jesus
"Blessed are the meek: for they shall inherit the earth."—Matthew 5:5

"The meek also shall increase their joy in the Lord, and the poor among men shall rejoice in the Holy One of Israel."—Isaiah 29:19

II. The _____ of Meekness

A. Meekness Properly Responds in _____
"To speak evil of no man, to be no brawlers, but gentle, shewing all meekness unto all men."—Titus 3:2

"But thou, O man of God, flee these things; and follow after righteousness, godliness, faith, love, patience, meekness."—1 TIMOTHY 6:11

B. Meekness Properly Responds in _____

"Likewise, ye wives, be in subjection to your own husbands; that, if any obey not the word, they also may without the word be won by the conversation of the wives; While they behold your chaste conversation coupled with fear. Whose adorning let it not be that outward adorning of plaiting the hair, and of wearing of gold, or of putting on of apparel; But let it be the hidden man of the heart, in that which is not corruptible, even the ornament of a **meek** *and quiet spirit, which is in the sight of God of great price."*
—1 PETER 3:1–4

C. Meekness Properly Responds in _____

"But sanctify the Lord God in your hearts: and be ready always to give an answer to every man that asketh you a reason of the hope that is in you with meekness and fear: Having a good conscience; that, whereas they speak evil of you, as of evildoers, they may be ashamed that falsely accuse your good conversation in Christ."—1 PETER 3:15–16

III. The _____ of Meekness

A. Meekness _____ Christ in You

"Take my yoke upon you, and learn of me; for I am meek and lowly in heart: and ye shall find rest unto

your souls. For my yoke is easy, and my burden is light."—MATTHEW 11:29–30

B. Meekness _____ the Word in You
"Wherefore lay apart all filthiness and superfluity of naughtiness, and receive with meekness the engrafted word, which is able to save your souls. But be ye doers of the word, and not hearers only, deceiving your own selves."—JAMES 1:21–22

Conclusion

Study Questions

1. Write the definition of meekness.

2. Who was the greatest example of meekness?

3. What does Psalm 25:9 say about the source of meekness?

4. Name the three services of meekness.

5. Since we cannot control the actions of others, what is in our power to control? Now, think about the last time you reacted in an unpleasing way. How could you have reacted in the spirit of meekness?

6. When witnessing to others, why is it important to have a spirit of meekness?

7. When somebody blatantly disagrees with our doctrine, someone without the spirit of meekness would distastefully argue and try to get their point across. What would a person with the spirit of meekness do?

8. One way to know you are manifesting meekness is if you are reflecting God's Word. Memorize these verses: James 1:21–22 and let it be your first step to placing meekness into your life.

Memory Verse

"The meek shall eat and be satisfied: they shall praise the LORD that seek him: your heart shall live for ever."—PSALM 22:26

The Fruit of Temperance

Text

Galatians 5:22–23; 1 Corinthians 9:24–27

Overview

The secret to self-control is giving Christ control. Achieving ultimate submission to our Lord's control can be done through the fruit of temperance. Temperance will help you in the areas of discipline and discretion—displaying itself in your speech, thoughts, and physical life. This lesson will take you step-by-step and show how you can practically develop temperance in your life.

Lesson Theme

The powerful fruit of temperance will develop self-control and discipline in the life of a yielded Christian in the areas of speech, thoughts, and physical life.

Introduction

_____

_____

_____

I. Temperance _____

A. *Self-Control,* _____
"*My son, let not them depart from thine eyes: keep sound wisdom and discretion: So shall they be life unto thy soul, and grace to thy neck. Then shalt thou walk in thy way safely, and thy foot shall not stumble.*"—PROVERBS 3:21–23

B. _____

II. Temperance _____

A. *A Disciplined* _____
"*But I keep under my body, and bring it into subjection....*"—1 CORINTHIANS 9:27

B. *A Disciplined* _____
"*Wherefore putting away lying, speak every man truth with his neighbor: for we are members one of another.*"—EPHESIANS 4:25

"*Let no corrupt communication proceed out of your mouth, but that which is good to the use of edifying, that it may minister grace unto the hearers.*"
—EPHESIANS 4:29

C. Disciplined _____

"Casting down imaginations, and every high thing that exalteth itself against the knowledge of God, and bringing into captivity every thought to the obedience of Christ;"—2 Corinthians 10:5

"Keep thy heart with all diligence; for out of it are the issues of life."—Proverbs 4:23

III. Temperance _____

A. Admit Your _____

"But every man is tempted, when he is drawn away of his own lust, and enticed. Then when lust hath conceived, it bringeth forth sin: and sin, when it is finished, bringeth forth death. Do not err, my beloved brethren."—James 1:14–16

B. Forget Your _____

"Brethren, I count not myself to have apprehended: but this one thing I do, forgetting those things which are behind, and reaching forth unto those things which are before, I press toward the mark for the prize of the high calling of God in Christ Jesus."—Philippians 3:13–14

C. Do Not Let Moods _____ You

"For the grace of God that bringeth salvation hath appeared to all men, Teaching us that, denying ungodliness and worldy lusts, we should live soberly, righteously, and godly, in this present world:"—Titus 2:11–12

D. Believe God Can Bring _____

"And be not conformed to this world: but be ye transformed by the renewing of your mind, that ye may prove what is that good, and acceptable, and perfect, will of God."—ROMANS 12:2

"I can do all things through Christ which strengtheneth me."—PHILIPPIANS 4:13

E. Become _____

"And if one prevail against him, two shall withstand him; and a threefold cord is not quickly broken."
—ECCLESIASTES 4:12

F. Avoid _____

"Be ye angry, and sin not: let not the sun go down upon your wrath: Neither give place to the devil."
—EPHESIANS 4:26–27

G. _____ on God's Power

"This I say then, Walk in the Spirit, and ye shall not fulfil the lust of the flesh. For the flesh lusteth against the Spirit, and the Spirit against the flesh: and these are contrary the one to the other: so that ye cannot do the things that ye would."
—GALATIANS 5:16–17

"For it is God which worketh in you both to will and to do of his good pleasure."—PHILIPPIANS 2:13

Conclusion

_____

_____

Study Questions

1. List the definitions given of temperance.

2. In what three areas will temperance display itself?

3. What are the four areas of speech every Christian should avoid?

4. What area of speech do you struggle with the most? Once you have pinpointed your weakest area in speech, claim and memorize one of the relating verses. (Ephesians 4:25, Ephesians 4:29, Proverbs 16:32, Proverbs 10:18)

5. What seven steps develop temperance?

6. A wrong act is thought about before it is ever committed. What wrong thoughts do you continually struggle with? What verse can you claim to help you with your thoughts in order to prevent them from becoming actions?

7. Read James 1:14–16 and write down the pattern of sin.

8. In what areas is your flesh battling to control instead of allowing the Holy Spirit to control?

Memory Verse

"Let no corrupt communication proceed out of your mouth, but that which is good to the use of edifying, that it may minister grace unto the hearers."—EPHESIANS 4:29

It Is Time

Text
Galatians 5:16; Ephesians 5:18

Overview
No more putting off the decision, the time has come! Will you choose to walk in the Spirit of God? If you do, a time of rejoicing, refreshing and revival will inevitably follow. As we conclude this series, allow this lesson to show you the blessings that come from living a life yielded to the Spirit.

Lesson Theme
When a Christian understands, accepts, and applies the truth of the person of the Holy Spirit and the fruit He produces, God rewards this decision through times of blessing.

Introduction

_____

_____

_____

I. A Time for _____

A. *Rejoice in* _____

"But I have trusted in thy mercy; my heart shall rejoice in thy salvation."—Psalm 13:5

"But whosoever drinketh of the water that I shall give him shall never thirst; but the water that I shall give him shall be in him a well of water springing up into everlasting life."—John 4:14

"Not by works of righteousness which we have done, but according to his mercy he saved us, by the washing of regeneration, and renewing of the Holy Ghost; Which he shed on us abundantly through Jesus Christ our Saviour."—Titus 3:5–6

B. *Rejoice in* _____

"In whom ye also trusted, after that ye heard the word of truth, the gospel of your salvation: in whom also after that ye believed, ye were sealed with that holy Spirit of promise, Which is the earnest of our inheritance until the redemption of the purchased possession, unto the praise of his glory."—Ephesians 1:13–14

"Who hath also sealed us, and given the earnest of the Spirit in our hearts."—2 Corinthians 1:22

II. A Time for _____

"Repent ye therefore, and be converted, that your sins may be blotted out, when the times of refreshing shall come from the presence of the Lord;"—ACTS 3:19

A. Refreshed by the _____ of the Spirit

"And I will pray the Father, and he shall give you another Comforter, that he may abide with you for ever; Even the Spirit of truth; whom the world cannot receive, because it seeth him not, neither knoweth him: but ye know him; for he dwelleth with you, and shall be in you."—JOHN 14:16–17

"Likewise the Spirit also helpeth our infirmities: for we know not what we should pray for as we ought: but the Spirit itself maketh intercession for us with groanings which cannot be uttered. And he that searcheth the hearts knoweth what is the mind of the Spirit, because he maketh intercession for the saints according to the will of God."—ROMANS 8:26–27

B. Refreshed by the _____ of the Spirit

"But the Comforter, which is the Holy Ghost, whom the Father will send in my name, he shall teach you all things, and bring all things to your remembrance, whatsoever I have said unto you."—JOHN 14:26

III. A Time for _____

A. _____ Revival

"Be not deceived; God is not mocked: for whatsoever a man soweth, that shall he also reap. For he that

soweth to his flesh shall of the flesh reap corruption; but he that soweth to the Spirit shall of the Spirit reap life everlasting. And let us not be weary in well doing: for in due season we shall reap, if we faint not."
—GALATIANS 6:7–9

B. _____ *Revival*

C. _____ *Revival*
"Wilt thou not revive us again: that thy people may rejoice in thee?"—PSALM 85:6

Conclusion

_____

_____

_____

"I Jesus have sent mine angel to testify unto you these things in the churches. I am the root and the offspring of David, and the bright and morning star. And the Spirit and the bride say, Come. And let him that heareth say, Come. And let him that is athirst come. And whosoever will, let him take the water of life freely."—REVELATION 22:16–17

Study Questions

1. How is the word *rejoicing* defined in this chapter?

2. What are the two areas you can rejoice in if you have the Holy Spirit inside of you?

3. Into what does the Holy Spirit guide you?

4. What is the best way to squelch revival in your family?

5. How can the comfort of the Holy Spirit refresh your soul?

6. How can you experience personal revival? What will
    you do to follow through?

7. What does it take to begin a revival in your own
    family?

8. Throughout this complete study, list the truths and
    principles that you have learned. List next to each truth
    what you will do to apply them to your life so that you
    might bear the fruit of the Spirit. How can you use
    these truths that God has given to you to help others?

Memory Verse

*"Wilt thou not revive us again: that thy people may rejoice in
thee?"*—PSALM 85:6

For additional Christian
growth resources visit
www.strivingtogether.com